LOCAL STUDIES
IN HISTORY AND
GEOGRAPHY

People and Journeys

Rosemary Rees

Janet Withersby

First published in Great Britain by Heinemann Library, Halley Court, Jordan Hill, Oxford OX2 8EJ
a division of Reed Educational and Professional Publishing Ltd

OXFORD FLORENCE PRAGUE MADRID ATHENS MELBOURNE AUCKLAND KUALA LUMPUR
SINGAPORE TOKYO IBADAN NAIROBI KAMPALA JOHANNESBURG GABORONE
PORTSMOUTH NH CHICAGO MEXICO CITY SAO PAULO

Designed by Aricot Vert Design

Illustrations by Sally Damant

Originated in the UK by Dot Gradations Ltd, Wickford

Printed in the UK by Jarrold Book Printing Ltd, Thetford

00 99 98 97 96

10 9 8 7 6 5 4 3 2 1

0 431 07893 9

British Library Cataloguing in Publication Data

Rees, Rosemary, 1942 –
    People and journeys – (Local studies in history and geography)
    1. Voyages and travels – Juvenile literature
    2. Geography – Juvenile literature
    I. Title II. Withersby, Janet
    910

Acknowledgements

The Publishers would like to thank the following for permission to reproduce photographs:
British Museum: p.26; Colyton Parish History Society: p.21; Dales Countryside Museums: p.15;
Mary Evans Picture Library: pp.9, 10, 12, 27; Images: pp.11, 14; Lancashire Library: pp.19, 28;
Ordnance Survey: pp.6, 7 16, 17, 22, 23, 28, 29; Science & Society Picture Library: p.13;
Roger Scruton: pp.3, 4, 18, 20, 24, 25; South Pennine Packhorse Trails: p.8

Cover photograph reproduced with permission of Zefa Picture Library (UK) Ltd.

Maps reproduced from Ordnance Survey mapping with the permission of The Controller
of Her Majesty's Stationery Office © Crown Copyright, Licence No. MC8575 OM.

Our thanks to Jane Shuter for her comments in the preparation of this book.

Every effort has been made to contact copyright holders of any material reproduced in this book.
Any omissions will be rectified in subsequent printings if notice is given to the Publisher.

Contents

Finding the way

How is your place connected to other places?

The road to everywhere begins at your own front door. You can travel to another part of the world or just around the corner.

Some of your journeys are everyday journeys. Do they take you along main roads? Do they take you along quiet streets or paths?

Which are the busiest main roads in your area? You could plan an investigation to find out. Can you think of reasons why these roads are the busiest? Think about where they go to, and why people might want to go there.

Recording roads

One of the best ways to record roads is to draw a map. How could you show which roads are the busiest? You could record where these roads go to on your map. You could also use your computer to record data about the roads you investigate.

Mark and Satveer are photographing road signs near their school. They are finding out how their place is connected to other places. You could collect information from road signs near you.

Old paths and old footprints

Look at the pictures on this page. Have you seen any footpath signs like these? Most footpaths are very old paths. Some are more than 2000 years old. They show us the everyday journeys made by people who lived in a place. Their feet began to wear away grass and soil. Soon their journeys had made footpaths.

We can still walk along some of these footpaths, but the wider routes have been covered by hard **tarmac**. They have become main roads, town roads and country lanes.

Finding out about old paths and roads

Your local history library might have maps which show what your place used to be like. If you live in a village, your roads and paths might not have changed very much. If you live in a town, you might find that your part of the town had fields and footpaths in the past.

If you find an old map, look at a house or farm. Where did footpaths take the people who lived there in the past?

These signs tell you where footpaths go. Why do you think people in the past needed to go to these places?

LOOK OUT

Look out for a 'Public Footpath' sign.

**Try to work out why the footpath is there.
If you would like to explore the footpath,
ask an adult in your family to go with you.**

Maps and patterns

Like the spokes of a wheel

Look at the lanes and footpaths on this map. Most of them meet in the village of Chipping. They look like bent spokes in an old bicycle wheel. This is called a **radial pattern**. The orange lanes are **surfaced** with **tarmac** and are wide enough for cars. The green dotted lines are footpaths.

At the centre, where ways meet

Way is an old word for road, footpath or lane. You will notice that many ways meet at a place where people go to church, school, the pub or post office. For hundreds of years people have come to the church, pub, or market. For hundreds of years people have set off from this centre to go to other places. Some ways meet at the place where the water-mill used to be. Farmers brought their corn to be ground here. On the map the mill is called 'Works'. It is now a chair factory.

Investigating village centres

If you live in a village, look at a map of your village. Where do most of the roads and footpaths meet? What is here? Why do people need to come to this place now? Why did they come here in the past?

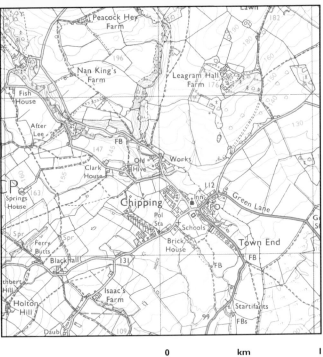

This map shows lanes and footpaths leading to the village of Chipping in Lancashire.

LOOK OUT

You can look at any map, from anywhere in the world and see road patterns.

If many roads and paths meet at the same place, many people must have travelled there.

Town patterns

Braintree is a larger place than Chipping. It is a town in Essex which has a busy town centre. Look at the roads on this map. They make a radial pattern like those in Chipping. But one road is different. It is a ring road which takes traffic round the edge of town. Motorists on the main roads can choose to drive into the town centre or round the outside of Braintree to other places.

The first roads

Braintree is at the crossroads of two Roman roads. Look at the map. Can you think which of the modern main roads have been built over the two Roman roads? Where do these roads meet? On the map red dotted lines are footpaths. Where do they go?

Investigating town centres

Look at a map of a town you know. Where do most of the roads meet? Find out what sort of buildings are there. Why do people come to this place?

Think about people who begin their journeys at the town centre. To which places do the main roads go? Can you find out what the town centre was like in the past, and why people went there?

This map shows the pattern of roads in Braintree, Essex.

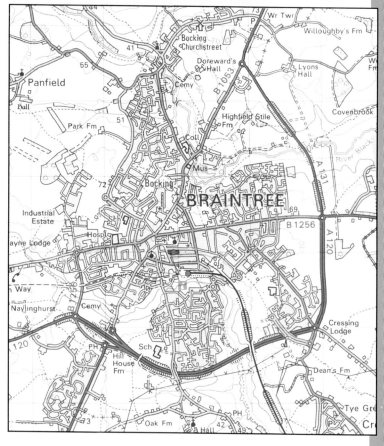

Bad roads and better roads

What were old roads like?

Do you live near a Roman road? When the Romans came to Britain over 2,000 years ago, they planned a **network** of main roads. They built hard roads with good stone **foundations**. Most other roads and tracks were worn by the walking feet of people and animals, and by the turning of wooden wheels.

Roads for feet and hooves

In the past, how did people travel around Britain? Until Victorian times, many travellers walked very long distances. Many people carried things to sell in packs on their backs. Some had **packhorses** who carried their loads in baskets, to markets far away. These baskets were called **panniers**, and loads were things like salt, wool, cloth, coal, iron, cheese and hay.

Drovers walked their animals to market. Many other people travelled on horseback.

These travellers could travel on broad roads or narrow paths between towns and villages. They could travel over the hills to avoid some of the really muddy places.

Roads for feet, hooves and wheels

Heavier loads were carried in carts and wagons, which were pulled by horses or **oxen**. Horses also pulled coaches. These wheeled vehicles had to travel on wider roads which were not too steep. It was hard for them to avoid the wet and muddy parts of these roads.

This engraving by an artist was made over 100 years ago. It shows how he imagined the packhorses looked more than 300 years before his time. Today, people ride horses along the old packhorse trails for fun.

This picture of a stagecoach at night was painted in 1839. The turnpike-keeper has got out of bed to open the gate. He is going to charge the coachman a toll to travel on the next part of the road.

Why did the roads become bad?

After the Roman army left Britain, there was no organized group of people to repair the hard Roman roads. Wheels made deep **ruts** in **soft roads**, and the ruts filled with rain water. More and more carts and wagons used the roads, and this made them worse.

By Tudor times, over 400 years ago, many roads could not be used in winter-time by wheeled traffic.

What did people do about the roads?

The people in each **parish** were responsible for repairing their own parts of the roads, but they did not always repair them well. Some travellers even drowned when they fell into holes in the road. More often, carts and carriages stuck in the mud. Sometimes their wooden wheels broke.

Paying for better roads

Just over 300 years ago, Parliament allowed private companies to own some of the main roads and to build gates or **turnpikes** across them. Travellers had to stop at these gates. They had to pay a **toll** for their vehicles and animals as they passed through. The money they paid was used to repair the road. But these roads did not really improve for another hundred years. Then new methods were used to build roads with strong stone foundations.

LOOK OUT

Look out for house names like Toll Bar Cottage or Turnpike Cottage.

Your library might have a map which shows the turnpiked roads in your area.

Waterways

Carrying heavy loads

It is much easier to pull or push heavy loads in a container which floats on water, than it is to push or pull heavy loads in a container with wheels over rough surfaces. You could try this experiment yourself. Roads in this country were very rough until modern times. Water journeys were often better.

People have always had to **transport** heavy loads. First they had to take raw materials to places where things were made. Next, the goods that were made had to be sent to markets and shops.

This painting shows a horse pulling a canal barge. It was painted over 200 years ago, not long after most canals were built.

Who used river transport?

People in the past used rivers whenever they could. Romans, Anglo-Saxons and Vikings all used rivers to transport heavy loads. They travelled as far up-river as they could in their shallow boats, so many of their **ports** were far inland.

Some of these river ports were still being used 250 years ago. But larger boats were needed to carry more goods, and most rivers were unreliable. Sometimes there was not enough water for larger boats to sail, or there was too much fast-flowing water, which could be dangerous. A few rivers are still used for transporting goods. Do you live near a river which has boats or ships for carrying people or goods?

Why did people want canals?

A canal is not like a river. It was made by people, and its water is controlled and reliable. It is a water highway and joins places where goods and people need to go.

Canals made changes

From the 1740s to the 1840s canals were built all over Britain. They joined up towns and villages, and they joined these places to sea ports.

Horses walked beside the canals, pulling **barges** loaded with coal and heavy goods. In some towns, new factories were built beside the canal. Near to the new factories, houses were built for workers to live in. These towns grew larger. People could travel on canals, too. Canal travel was smoother than road travel.

Investigating canals

Is there a canal near you? Does it begin at a sea port? Through which towns does it travel? You might be able to find out what the canal barges used to carry and how this helped people in your area. You could make drawings or take photographs of old canal-side buildings and bridges. Try to find out how the canal is used today.

This modern photograph shows part of the Oxford Canal at Napton-on-the-Hill in Warwickshire. You can see a 'staircase' of locks which bring the barges down the hill.

LOOK OUT

*If you visit a canal look out for **locks**.*

Try to work out how locks help boats to travel up or down hill.

Steam power

Moving steam engines

In the 1780s people began to use steam engines to power machines in factories. Coal fires boiled water to make the steam which powered the engines. Steam engines made machines work faster. When ships began to be powered by steam engines, sea journeys became faster. People began to experiment with steam engines to pull trucks along smooth iron rails. At first, these steam trains on railway lines only moved heavy things like coal or stone. By the 1820s, people began to think how railways might be more useful.

This picture was painted in about 1850. A train has just arrived at this new railway station. How have people managed to bring their carriages with them?

Who wanted railways?

Railway trains could travel faster than canal **barges**. Anyone who wanted faster **transport** wanted railways.

Businessmen who owned factories needed faster transport. They wanted railways to link their factories to other places.

Trains could bring heavy materials to the factories. They could take goods from the factories to town markets to be sold in Britain. They could take goods to **ports** too, to be **exported** to places all over the world.

Coal-mine owners wanted to send heavy loads of coal to factories quickly. Farmers wanted railways to take food and milk quickly from their farms to the town's shops.

Working people wanted railways. They discovered that railway travel was going to be cheap enough for many of them to save up for trips to the seaside, the country or large towns.

Businessmen and people who owned land near the sea wanted to make these places into new seaside resorts and ports. Railways could bring people and goods to these places.

Wealthy people wanted to travel more quickly and comfortably. Some wanted to move out of the town and live in the countryside, but still be able to travel quickly to work in the town.

What sort of people might have wanted a railway in the place where you live?

Who did not want railways?

People who earned money from canal transport and **toll** collectors on the **turnpiked** roads did not want railways. Neither did people who ran stage coaches or who hired horses to road travellers. They were all worried that the railway might be a success and people would stop using their kind of transport. Do you know if there were once people like these where you live?

This poster tells you about a grand day-trip on a train in Victorian times. It shows you a picture of a train at this time. Where could people go on this train and what could they do there?

There were also people who were afraid that railway trains would be dangerous for people and for the animals in fields near railway lines.

Railways arrive

Railway companies were formed and plans were made. By the 1850s most towns and many villages in Britain were linked by railway lines. Factories were built in towns where there were railways and plenty of people to work.

Lancashire and Yorkshire Railway.

GRAND DAY TRIP
On Monday, August 6th,
TO
BLACKPOOL

ALTHAM'S TRIP ON ABOVE DATE LEAVES a.m.

Burnley (Bank Top) 6-30

Burnley (Barracks) 6-35

Returning from Blackpool (Talbot Road) at 6-50 p.m.

FARE  3/-

Those going by my Trip to Blackpool will be admitted to the North Pier there (which is now the finest in the world), on payment of 1d. for a Special Ticket, which can be obtained at time of purchasing their Railway Ticket. The usual charge for each person is 2d.

Tickets can be had at my Establishment,

MARKET PLACE, BURNLEY.

ABM. ALTHAM,
Wholesale and Retail Tea Merchant.

George Frankland, Printer, &c., Bull Street, Burnley.

Railways today

What are railway stations like today?

Is there a railway station where you live? Do you know how old it is? If you live near a large station it might have a fast-food bar, shops and toilets. There might be electronic timetables above the platforms. If you live near a small station you might not see many of these things. Perhaps it has only two platforms and a printed timetable.

Where do trains go to from here?

Think about your nearest railway station. Do the trains take people to towns, cities, **ports**, or to seaside resorts? You could look at a map to find out. Trains might bring people from other places to the town where they work. Other trains might take people to places for their shopping. Do you ever travel by train? Where do you go to?

This photograph shows St Pancras Station in London. It was built in the 1860s for Victorian travellers. It is still a busy station today.

LOOK OUT

Most railway stations were built about 150 years ago. Some stations still have old Victorian buildings.

Victorian builders used patterns to decorate their buildings. Look out for patterns on old station buildings.

Buildings beside the railway

If your home or school is near a railway line, look around. Can you see any buildings which might have been built to be near the railway? There might be old factory buildings which were built because heavy loads could be delivered easily by train. There might be houses which were built for the people who worked in the factories.

Places without railways

If you have no railway station near you, try to find out who has lived in this place for a long time. They might be able to tell you if there was an old station here. Many railway lines and hundreds of stations were closed in the 1960s.

At that time the government decided there were not enough passengers travelling on the trains.

Looking for lost railways

If your village or town once had a railway station, you might be able to discover where it was and what has happened to it. Some of the buildings might still be there, or perhaps new buildings have been built on this site. Sometimes the old railway line has been made into a place to walk.

This photograph shows an old railway station which was closed years ago. It is now used as a farming museum.

Railways and **new roads**

People on the move

The small town of Harlow in Essex began to change in the 1950s. Thousands of new homes were needed for people from London, so a **new town** was built at Harlow. Some people who came to live in Harlow worked there, too. But some people still travelled to London to work.

Reading maps

The map on this page was made in the 1950s. The map on the next page was made in the 1990s. They both show Harlow. We can compare the maps to see if there have been any changes to the roads and railways.

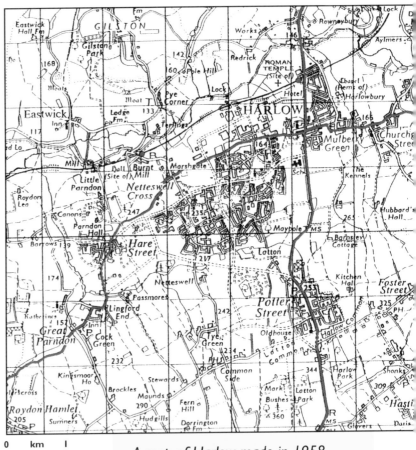

A map of Harlow made in 1958.

Do people still travel by train?

The railway line to London is shown on the maps as a bold black line with red circles for the stations. Find the railway line and the stations on the 1958 map. Look at the 1992 map. Do you think people still use the railway today?

What were the main roads like in the 1950s?

There were only two main roads through Harlow in the 1950s. Find them on the map. They are coloured red.

LOOK OUT

Do people in your family use cars more than they used to?

Ask older people in your family how they travelled to school, town or the shops when they were younger.

What are the main roads like in the 1990s?

Look for red main roads on this map. Can you work out which are the old main roads? How many new main roads can you find?

When were the new roads made?

Look at the 1958 map. Find some roads shown as double rows of dotted lines. These are places where road-building had begun. But the roads were not finished when the map was made.

Why did Harlow need more new roads?

In the 1950s, some families had a car, but most people travelled on buses or trains, or cycled to work and to the shops. Now, many families have two cars. New roads were needed for all the extra cars and delivery lorries.

Transporting heavy loads

Trains used to carry more **freight** in the 1950s. Now lorries carry freight on motorways and wide main roads. A motorway was built which joined Harlow to London. Can you find the motorway on this map? It is coloured blue.

A map of Harlow in 1992.

0   km   1

More cars and **lorries**

Why are there more cars on the roads?

Since the 1950s more people have become car owners. They use their cars for most of their everyday journeys. Lorries have become larger and heavier since the 1950s, too.

How have cars and lorries changed towns?

More cars and lorries need more road space. New roads might have been built where you live. Perhaps old roads have been widened from two lanes to three or four lanes.

In town centres, roads cannot be made wider because of all the buildings. Some roads are closed to traffic, and have become **pedestrian precincts**. Traffic is only allowed to travel one way along some narrow town-centre roads. Roundabouts, traffic lights and **fly-overs** are often used to keep the extra traffic moving smoothly and safely. Most towns have lots of road signs to help motorists find their way around. Car parks are built to provide parking spaces for people who come to town in a car.

LOOK OUT

Has traffic made changes to the place where you live? You might know someone with old photographs of this place. Find out how many changes have been made because of cars and lorries.

This photograph of the Market Car Park in Curzon Street, in Burnley, was taken in 1995. It covers a huge area of land in the town centre.

How have cars changed villages?

New roads and motorways make changes to some villages. They cut through the fields, woods and footpaths nearby. Sometimes houses and farm buildings are **demolished** to make way for new roads.

Some families buy houses in villages because a new motorway or fast road makes it possible to live in the country but work in the town.

Do villages need car parks?

Many villages now need car parks. Some villages have a village centre with shops, a church, school, pub and perhaps a village hall. People who live on farms, or on a new housing estate outside the village centre, come to the village centre in their cars. **Tourists** who visit the village need car parks too.

What can we find out from old photographs?

The photograph on this page was taken in 1968. It shows shops and a cotton mill in Burnley which were demolished to make space for the Market Car Park.

Can this really be the same place as that shown on the other photograph? Look at the building on the right edge of the 1968 photograph. Can you find it on the 1995 photograph?

This photograph of Curzon Street in 1968 was taken from the same place as the 1995 photograph on page 18.

Colyton: a meeting place

Why did people come to Colyton?

Colyton is a village in Devon. Historians think that a group of Anglo-Saxon people came across the sea to the mouth of the River Coly, and travelled beside the river for about three miles. They chose a large area of land for themselves and built their main village beside the river.

This photograph shows the Chantry Bridge at Colyton. There is another bridge in the village where the River Coly meets the River Umbourne. One summer day in 1968, the river overflowed its banks and washed a house away.

This was Colyton. It was the main meeting place for a group of ten villages. People built a church and held a market and a fair there.

Using photographs as evidence

This photograph was taken in Colyton. You can discover some things about this place from the photograph. You can see the River Coly. Do you think the river is deep or shallow? Why do you think there is a bridge there? Does this photograph help you find any reasons why the village was chosen as the meeting place for people from the other nine villages, too?

This is a postcard of Colyton Fair, in 1908.

Finding out from old photographs

The photograph on this page is a postcard of Colyton. Postcards are useful because there is usually some writing on them to tell you about the picture. You could use old postcards to find out about the place where you live.

Looking and thinking

What sort of people can you see in this photograph? What do you think is happening here? Why do you think there is a cow in the centre of the circle? What is happening behind the circle? Can you think of any reasons why so many people were in Colyton market-place? Where do you think all the people came from?

Using other evidence

A historian read the old market records of Colyton and discovered that the Colyton Cattle Fair was held every Thursday and every Saturday until 1920. Does this evidence help you to decide what is happening in the photograph?

LOOK OUT

Is there a market where you live? There might have been a market long ago. Look out for road names with 'market' in them. Market Street in Manchester, and Haymarket in London used to be market places.

Colyton: journeys

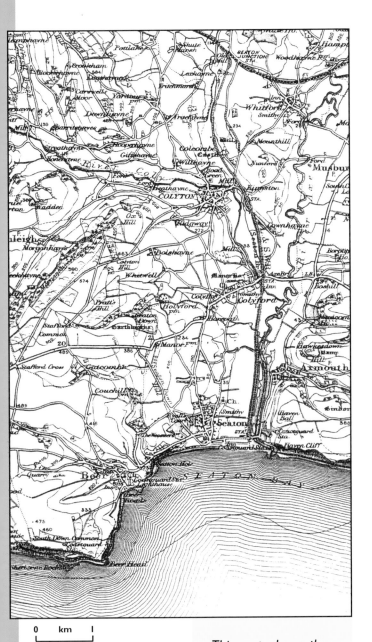

This map shows the area around Colyton in 1893.

0   km   I

Discovering old journeys on a map

Look at the map on this page. The red dotted lines are footpaths. Most of the footpaths and lanes meet at Colyton. People in the past travelled here on foot, horseback or the **wheeled transport** of their time.

Railways arrive

The map on this page was made in the 1890s. Find a railway line at the top of the map. This part of the railway went from London to Exeter. It was built in 1860.

Railways made changes

Before the railway came, there were many small places with markets like Colyton in the county of Devon. There were also many fishing villages along the sea coast.

When the railway came it brought people to Devon who wanted seaside holidays. It also made changes for people who lived in Devon's villages. They began to travel on trains to big towns where there were more shops and larger markets. During the railway age fewer people came to small markets like Colyton.

This map shows the area around Colyton in 1992.

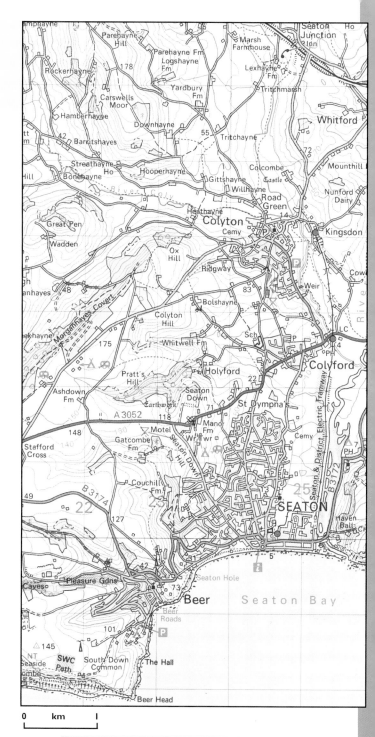

A line to the seaside

A junction is a place where two railways join. Look at the 1890s map. Can you find Seaton Junction? Can you see another railway line going from Seaton Junction to the seaside village of Seaton? It was built to bring holiday visitors to Seaton. The map-maker wrote 'STA' by every railway station. Where did the trains stop?

Does Colyton have a main road?

The map on this page was made in the 1990s. Look at the red main roads. No modern main roads pass through Colyton. But a long time ago, it was the most important village in the area. Even when Victoria was queen the roads to Colyton were not busy enough to be made into main roads. (See the map made in 1893.) Why do you think they were not busy?

Which is the busiest road today?

The modern main road crosses the river at Colyford. Lots of people and traffic travel along this road between the seaside towns along the coast and the large town of Exeter. People who live in country villages use this road to travel to Exeter.

LOOK OUT

Look at the seaside place called Seaton on the 1893 and 1992 maps. What has happened to Seaton since the railway began to bring holiday visitors here?

Colyton: a place to visit

Who comes to Colyton now?

Tourists come to visit Colyton in the summer when they are on holiday in Devon. It is a pretty village, full of old and interesting buildings. Do you live in a town or village which tourists visit?

Who wants them to come?

People who own shops, cafés, restaurants and small hotels in Colyton want tourists to come and spend money. So do the owners of the caravan parks. They have had advertisements made to tell people that they would enjoy themselves if they came to Colyton.

Class 4 time detectives

In 1991 the children in Class 4 at Colyton Primary School investigated the buildings in their village. They recorded what they discovered on their computer and **typeset** their own *History Trail* booklet. A firm of printers in Colyford printed the booklets. Now visitors to Colyton can buy these booklets and learn all about the village buildings as they walk round. The children have helped to make Colyton interesting for tourists.

This photograph shows Colyton Railway Station. Once steam trains stopped here. Now it is a tramway for old trams. What else can people do at Colyton station?

This photograph shows the bus that goes to Seaton seafront. It is picking up passengers in Colyton. Many people who live here travel to other towns in their own cars. They can also drive to catch a train at Axminster Station which is about 7 kilometres away.

What happened to the railway?

Look at the map on page 23. Can you see what has happened to the railway line between Seaton and Seaton Junction? If you read the writing beside the track you will discover more. The railway closed in 1965 because there were not enough passengers. Many people came on holiday in their own cars.

New ideas and old trams

A group of people who were interested in old trams thought of a way of using the old railway line and stations. They decided to run old trams on the line. Now, seaside holiday-makers at Seaton can have an exciting trip to Colyton on an old tram. Seventy-two thousand people travelled on the Seaton Tramway in 1995.

Who visits your place?

Find out what people can do if they visit your town or village. Your local Tourist Information Centre or library will have leaflets about interesting places and events.

LOOK OUT

Is there a place near you that might interest tourists or people who live nearby?

Perhaps you could find out more about it and make a booklet for tourists.

Burnley: old journeys

Why did people come here?

Burnley is a town in Lancashire. Long ago, Anglo-Saxon people chose a place to live near Burnley. Later, Burnley became the main village in the area. About 700 years ago there was already a market, a church, and two water mills beside the river.

This picture was painted in 1814. It shows men and their packhorses carrying woollen cloth over the hills to sell in cloth markets in Yorkshire.

Cloth-makers came to Burnley

One of those mills in Burnley was called a **fulling mill**. Most people in this area made cloth from greased wool on looms in their homes. The cloth had to be cleaned before it could be sold. People came from far away to have their cloth washed at Burnley fulling mill, and to sell their washed cloth at Burnley market.

How did people travel here?

Most people walked to Burnley, and many walked with their **packhorses**. The packhorses carried heavy loads of coal, lime and cloth, as well as many other things.

This drawing shows two coal-miners at work in the 1840s.

Some people drove animals to market. Some travelled on horseback and others came with carts and wagons pulled by horses or oxen. On market days and fair days they came to buy and sell. They also came to have their corn ground at the other mill and to hear the news.

Coal journeys

Coal-mining really began in Burnley in Tudor times. Coal-miners dug small coal mines in the ground. They loaded coal into basket **panniers** strapped to the backs of their packhorses. The horses were led along **bridleways** and lanes to customers at farms, houses, workshops, **forges** and **kilns**. Later, when coal was used in the steam powered cotton mills, coal-mines became much larger and deeper.

Canal journeys

About 200 years ago a canal was built through Burnley. People came from nearby villages and places further away to work as canal builders. They were called **navvies**. When the canal was finished, some of them stayed to work in the cotton mills in Burnley. Some families lived most of their lives on canal boats, carrying heavy loads along the canal.

Families on the move

In Victorian times people came to live in Burnley from many towns and villages. They came to find work in the cotton mills and coal-mines of Burnley. In the 1830s poor families from the south of England travelled on canal barges all the way from London. In the 1840s some people came over the hills from Yorkshire, or across the sea from Ireland on ships. Since the 1960s, families have come over the sea in aeroplanes from India or Pakistan. For many of these families, Burnley is now their home.

Burnley: **clues** from **maps**

Making the map

The map on this page was made by a man called Christopher Greenwood in 1818. No one had made a map of Burnley since 1784.

There had been a lot of changes. A canal had been built through the town, more cotton mills had been built, and the town had grown larger. The information on the 1784 map was not right any more. Christopher Greenwood needed to record changes on his new map.

Reading the map

He drew the canal on the map with a bold black line. It makes two sides of a triangle as it travels round Burnley. Can you find it?

The **turnpiked** roads are the widest roads and have a bold black line drawn along one edge. How many turnpiked roads came from other towns to Burnley?

Can you see all the buildings in the old town of Burnley? They are the small black rectangles beside the bend in the river, where all the roads meet.

This map of Burnley was made in 1818. It is part of Christopher Greenwood's map of Lancashire.

Finding out from the map

Historians say that Burnley began to grow after the canal was built. You can check this yourself. Look at the map. Have any buildings been built beside the new canal or along the turnpiked roads, away from the town centre?

LOOK OUT

Look for the word 'Bar' on the map. These are places where there was a toll bar or turnpike.

Look at page 9 to find out what sort of vehicles travelled along the turnpiked roads.

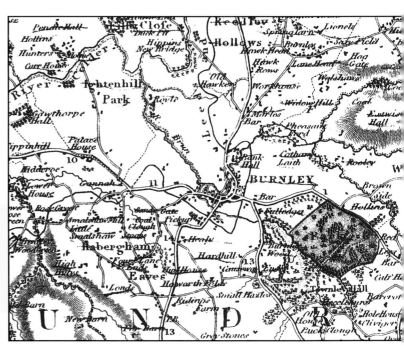

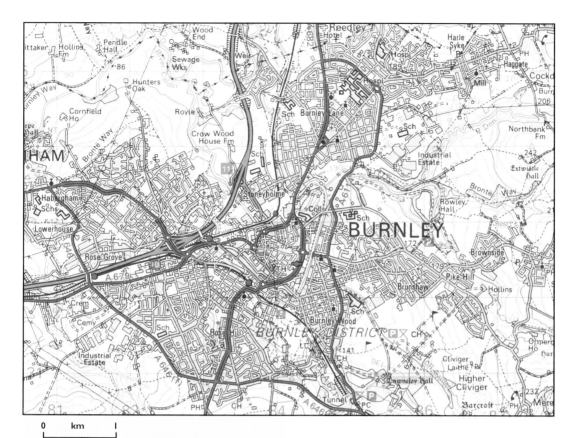

0   km   l

This is a map of Burnley. It was made by the Ordnance Survey in 1994. There is a map like this of the place where you live. Have you had a chance to look at it?

Did Burnley grow?

This map was made in the 1990s. The area covered by houses and buildings is coloured pink. Compare it with the map on the opposite page to see how Burnley has grown. If you do not believe that the maps show the same place, look for the shape made by the canal on both maps.

Railway journeys

The railway arrived here in the 1840s. It linked Burnley to the port of Liverpool, the town of Manchester, and all the industrial and seaside towns in Lancashire and Yorkshire. In Victorian times the railway was important to people who lived and worked in Burnley. It is still used today. Count how many stations you can see on this map. They are small red circles.

Modern journeys

If you go to Burnley today you can go by train, or along the M65 motorway. You can travel along modern roads which have been built over the old turnpiked roads. You could travel along the canal in a pleasure boat, or walk along old footpaths with new names like the Pendle **Way**. You might drive through the town on new roads and **fly-overs**. Do you live in a town like Burnley?

Glossary

barge a boat built for carrying large amounts of heavy goods in shallow water

bridleways a path for horses and riders

demolished knocked down

drover a person whose job it was to walk animals from farms to faraway markets, along wide, grassy roads or tracks

exported sent to buyers in other countries

fly-over a main road which travels over the top of other roads on long bridges, so that the traffic on the main road does not have to stop at lots of crossroads

forge a place where a blacksmith makes things by heating metal and hammering it into shape

foundations layers of stone under the surface of the road. They make the road very hard and last a long time.

freight heavy loads, such as coal, new cars and food, being taken from factories to shops; also, animals being taken to cattle markets

fulling mill a water mill where the turning water wheel made large wooden hammers move up and down in a tub full of water and new cloth. This washed the grease out of the cloth.

kiln a place where grain was dried over a fire, or limestone was heated

locks a part of a canal which can be closed off from the rest of the canal by huge gates in the water. The gates allow the water to be raised or lowered, so that boats can float up to a higher part of the canal or down to a lower part.

navvies this is short for navigator, a name for people who built navigations or canals

network lines which touch other lines, like a net

new town a town of new houses and workplaces in the country, for families who used to live in crowded cities

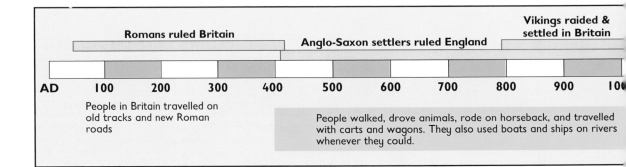

		Romans ruled Britain				Anglo-Saxon settlers ruled England				Vikings raided & settled in Britain

AD	100	200	300	400	500	600	700	800	900	100

People in Britain travelled on old tracks and new Roman roads

People walked, drove animals, rode on horseback, and travelled with carts and wagons. They also used boats and ships on rivers whenever they could.

oxen strong bulls who could pull heavy loads

packhorses horses which carry heavy loads in two packs, or baskets, on their backs, one on each side of the saddle

panniers the packs or baskets which the packhorses carried

parish each county, like Lancashire and Devon, is divided into areas called parishes. Each parish has its own church.

pedestrian precinct a road in a town centre which is for people only and cars and lorries are not allowed to use it

port a place where ships from other places can load and unload their cargoes

radial pattern this is like the shape you see when you look at the spokes and tyre of a bicycle wheel, with lines running from the centre to the edge

ruts long, deep cuts made by cart, wagon and coach wheels turning in soft soil or mud as they travel along

soft roads roads which have a soil surface and not a hard stone or tarmac surface

surfaced covered

tarmac this is short for tar macadam, which was the name given to a way of making a hard surface on a road. The road was covered with hot tar, and the tar was covered with tiny stones.

toll the money people pay so that they can travel along a road or across a bridge

tourist a person who visits a place for a holiday or day out

transport to carry from one place to another

turnpike a gate or bar across a road which makes travellers stop and pay a toll

typeset typing or setting out words which are going to be printed

way a Saxon word which was the most common word used in England for roads and paths, until long after Tudor times

wheeled transport any transport with wheels, such as carts, wagons, coaches, cars, lorries and bicycles

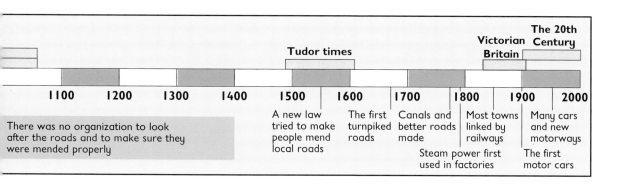

Tudor times

Victorian Britain

The 20th Century

| 1100 | 1200 | 1300 | 1400 | 1500 | 1600 | 1700 | 1800 | 1900 | 2000 |

There was no organization to look after the roads and to make sure they were mended properly

A new law tried to make people mend local roads

The first turnpiked roads

Canals and better roads made

Steam power first used in factories

Most towns linked by railways

Many cars and new motorways

The first motor cars

Index

Numbers in plain type (27) refer to the text. Numbers in italic type (27) refer to a caption or a picture.